HONNEY LAVERN BARNER

I am Amazing Grace

Revelation Knowledge

First published by HLB Hour Glass Publishing 2020

Copyright © 2020 by Honney Lavern Barner

All rights reserved. No part of this publication may be reproduced, stored or transmitted in any form or by any means, electronic, mechanical, photocopying, recording, scanning, or otherwise without written permission from the publisher. It is illegal to copy this book, post it to a website, or distribute it by any other means without permission.

This novel is entirely a work of fiction. The names, characters and incidents portrayed in it are the work of the author's imagination. Any resemblance to actual persons, living or dead, events or localities is entirely coincidental.

First edition

ISBN: ISBN: 978-1-952321-00-9

This book was professionally typeset on Reedsy.
Find out more at reedsy.com

Contents

About the Author — iv
Dedication — vi
Acknowledgements — vii
Books to Consider — viii
Prologue — x
Chapter 1 — 1
  A Safe Place — 1
Chapter 2 — 4
  Family Woes — 4
Chapter 3 — 8
  Keep your head up — 8
Chapter 4 — 11
  Change is coming — 11
Chapter 5 — 14
  It's Ok to be different — 14
Chapter 6 — 17
  Joy cometh in the morning — 17
Chapter 7 — 21
  We have another home — 21
Epilogue — 25
  Revelation Knowledge Changes Things! So, Change — 25
Other books by Dr. Honney Lavern Barner — 27
How you can help spread the word? — 29
Word of Mouth Matters - Your Help Matters — 30
Follow Dr. Honney Lavern Barner on Social Media — 33

About the Author

Dr. H. L. Barner grew up in Portsmouth, Virginia. His life started with a very humble beginning. Growing up without his Father he looked to his mother and grandfather for moral and spiritual guidance. He also received alot of encouragement, motivation, inspiration, and support from his oldest brother, teachers, community professionals, and his athletic coaches. His mother eventually led him to Jesus Christ and his grandfather continued to encourage his spiritual journey. After the death of his grandfather he committed himself to continue his spiritual journey. As a young adult, he developed a passion for attending different churches and local revivals. He enjoyed the preaching and teaching of the Gospel of Jesus Christ and was determined to learn everything he could about Him.

Several years later his passion led him to read the entire bible from cover to cover. He made a promise to God that he would introduce Jesus Christ to his son and any future children. As a new father he read the entire bible to his son and when his son came to age, his son read the entire bible to him. Dr. Barner later completed his course work with the Institute of Biblical Studies as well as Evangelist Training through Mercy Street Ministries. He enjoyed talking to people about the Lord and leading them to Christ. Throughout his early life he frequently offered rides to hitchhikers and ministers. He welcomed Mormons, Catholics, Jehovah Witnesses, and any one else into his home to discuss their faith and understanding of the bible. He volunteered as a Sunday school teacher at his local church as well hosting noontime bible study at work. Revelation is his favorite book of the bible.

H. L. continued his education by completing a Doctorate Degree of Theology in Biblical Studies. Through his twenty years of military service, H.L. traveled all around the world; however, his most exciting trip was to the Holy Land. He visited all the key biblical cities and sites such as Jerusalem, the Waling Wall, Capernaum, Jericho, the Temple Mount, Mount of Olive, Pool of Bethesda, Canaan, Gethsemane, Galilee, and Golgotha (Calvary Hill). During his visit, he sailed on the Sea of Galilee, floated in salty Dead Sea, swam in the Mediterranean, and was baptized in the Jordan River. He brought home bottles of water he personally extracted from the bodies of water above, collected leafs and branches from 2000 year old Olive trees as well as rocks from the location where it is prophesied that the world war known as "Armageddon" and the second coming of Jesus Christ will be. The most exciting portion of his trip was when a Palestinian local snuck him and another American minister, under the cloud of darkness, in to the town of Bethlehem in order to visit the basement of the church (the Holy sepulcher) where it is said to be the place where Jesus Christ was born. The experience from this trip gave him an entirely new outlook on life. Today when he reads the bible the places he is reading about comes to life because he has been there and experienced it for himself.

He is currently enrolled in another Doctorate Degree program studying the Theology of Jesus Christ and writing a four novel series entitled "Behind the Door". He has published the first two novels, Behind the Door, the Secrets to the Beginning and Behind the Door II, Revelation Revealed. Behind the Door III & IV are projected to be published in 2021 & 2022 respectively.

Dedication

I am Amazing Grace - Revelation Knowledge – for Young Adults….. is dedicated to:

Jesus Christ, My Lord and Savior

To every teenager and young adult developing their relationship with God.

To every teenager and young adult that do not know Jesus Christ as their Lord and Savior.

To every parent who has a teenager and/or young adult that need a word that will change their lives.

Acknowledgements

I acknowledge God, and that He is God all by Himself; He is the Creator of the world; He is the Alpha and Omega; He is the first and the last; He is the beginning and the end; He is the God of Gods, Lord of Lords, King of Kings; He is the God of Abraham, the God of Isaac, and the God of Jacob; He is the God of Israel; He is the Great "I AM".

I acknowledge Jesus Christ as my Lord and my Savior.

I acknowledge the Holy Spirit as my Guide and my Comforter.

I acknowledge all the designers, editors, and advisors of all my books and buks for their amazing talent, commitment to perfection, dedication unlike anything I have ever experienced. For their steady inspiration and motivation to see and understand my vision for these novels, books & buks.

I acknowledge all the readers of my other books and buks such as Let's Be Honest about MLM/Network Marketing, Behind the Door I – The Secrets to the Beginning. Thanks for making my very first novel an Amazon Best Seller, Most Gifted, and #1 Released. Let's do it again with Behind the Door, II, III, & IV – Revelation Revealed; Welcome to Heaven and Revelation Unleashed.

I acknowledge all the venues, businesses, churches, universities and homes that invited me to come share my story and hosted book signings.

I acknowledge all the guests on my weekly Podcast "Dr. Barner's Hour of Power."

Books to Consider

All rights reserved.

This buk is a work of fiction. All characters, names, locations and references are a part of the author's imagination. Any similarities are purely coincidental. Scriptures and other bible quotes come from the Kings James Version.

Contact Dr. Honney Lavern Barner
   Email: Behindthedoor2018@gmail.com

Other Books you will love to read:
   Let's Be Honest about MLM/Network Marketing (Released - 2014)
   Behind the Door: The Secrets to the Beginning (Released - 2018)
   Behind the Door II: Revelation Revealed (Released - 2019)
   Behind the Door III: Welcome to Heaven (Release - 2021)
   Behind the Door IV: Revelation Unleashed (Release - 2022)

Coming Soon: Pocket Buks by HLB Hour Glass Publishing
   Featuring my first but "I Let's be Honest about Network Marketing/MLM And now " I AM AMAZING GRACE"

All Pocket Buks are published by HLB Hour Glass Publishing. What are Pocket Buks? They are small but powerful books that will inspire, motivate, and educate readers. They are written to provide you information that is quickly read, easily understood and to the point. Most of these Pocket Buks can be read in 1 to 2 hour or less.

They are written for you.

Fill free to download and ebooks/ebuks and give them as gifts to your friends and family

For more information contact us: behindthedoor2018@gmail.com

Prologue

I am Amazing Grace || Revelation Knowledge – *for Young Adults*

"It is impossible to know what you do not know"

The goal of this book is to provide you with "Revelation Knowledge" about who you are in Christ Jesus using two of God's must amazing creations, the chicken and the eagle.

I am hoping by learning and coming to a full and perfect understanding about who you are, what you are, and why you are…. will ignite a Holy Ghost Fire inside you.

To live in God's eternal Kingdom with him forever and ever we must be Saved, Redeemed, Sanctified/Holy, Righteous, and Loved by God. If you have called on the mighty and powerful name of Jesus and you have committed your Body, Soul, and Spirit to Jesus, then you are saved.

What do these powerful life changing words mean:

1. **To be Saved** – Christians describe this phenomenon of gaining faith in Jesus Christ. It is an experience when everything they have been taught as Christians becomes real, and they develop a direct and personal relationship with God. You have eternal life with God.
2. **To be Redeemed** - In Christian theology, redemption refers to the deliverance of Christians from your past, present, and future sins. You are forgiven.

3. **To be Sanctified** - means basically 'you are set apart', in the sense of being set apart from all else and dedicated for God's purpose. This work of grace at salvation sets the believer apart as separate from and holy unto God. You are worthy.
4. **To be Righteous** - A righteous person not only does the right thing for other people but also follows the gospel of Jesus Christ.

If you do not know Jesus Christ as your Lord and Savior, simply from your heart and from wherever you are repeat the "Sinner's Prayer" below Romans 10:9.

When you are done the Angels in Heaven will celebrate and your name will be "permanently" recorded in Heaven for all eternity and no one will ever be able to reverse your new and awesome relationship with Jesus Christ. You have a new address in Heaven.

Now, what is next? Visit a few churches in your community, pray to God to direct your path in selecting your local church home. Once you join a bible teaching church in your area they will disciple you and provide the rest of the wonderful story of the Gospel of Jesus Christ found in the four Gospels - Matthew, Mark, Luke, and John. In fact, you don't have to wait. Download the Bible App on your phone and start reading today. Send me an email to let me know about the best decision you could ever make at behindthedoor2018@gmail.com.

Repeat: Romans 10:9 – "That is thou confess with thy mouth the Lord Jesus, and shalt believe in thine heart that God hath raised him from the dead, thou shalt be saved"

Mankind, at one point in time wanted to work and earn their way to God. The laws/commandments were given to us by God but used as a school master to show us that no man could not ever fulfill every law. No number of sacrifices with cleaned and/or uncleaned animals, feast, festivals, or worship could ever be enough.

So, God sent his only Son Jesus Christ to do what no man could do.

Born of a virgin Mother, died on Cavalry Cross, buried in a borrowed tomb, and raised from the dead by the Most High God.

He fulfilled every law. His last words on the cross was "It is finished".

He loved us first. We now live under GRACE. We have His MERCY.

The only thing for you to do is to have FAITH AND BELIEVE!

Why are we discussing Faith? Faith is not something you develop to impress God. Nor to get him to do something for us; nor get Him to love us more; absolutely not. Allow me to let you in on a very power revelation that most adults do not get or understand. Faith is the gift God gave us also to get us to take action; to move you and not Him. God has done everything for us. We must access everything through faith. Again, please understand that the one thing that empower Christians is faith. Most Christians are praying for faith to accomplish things. Well, if the truth is to be told everything is here and all we have to do is take action, go after it (execute our faith). I will come back to faith in another book.

Again, If you have received Jesus Christ as your Lord and Savior then you are the child of the Most High God. There is good news for you today. That good news is the Gospel of Jesus Christ.

What that means is that because of the life, death, and resurrection of Jesus Christ you are saved, redeemed, sanctified/holy, righteous, and loved by God and have eternal life with God our Father. Read: 1 Corinthians 1:30.

There is nothing you have done that earned these FREE gifts. There is nothing you can do to earn these FREE gifts. Jesus has done it all. And by the way, there is nothing you can do to lose His love either.

Many if not most Christians do not know nor are they sure if all these gifts are FREE and that they comes with the salvation and promise of God. Well, for the record....the answer is YES...they all come in one package!

"If you confess with your mouth, believe in your heart that God raised Jesus from the dead, you shall be saved". Remember I stated that before. Don't ever forget **Romans 10:9.** Because we live in a body and is still subject to sin (but we are no longer sinners) the enemy will tell you different and make you feel unworthy; make no doubt about it the enemy knows if you feel unworthy.

With that being said, let's begin with this story in which I believe will answer and reveal unto you exactly who you are. After you finish reading this buk you will be very excited and thankful to God for allowing you to know and enjoy this awesome "Revelation Knowledge" that Amazing Grace discovered during the lowest time in his life.

The story, well it is......you will get my point after you finished reading.

1 John 3: 2 - 8

Dear friends, now we are children of God, and what we will be has not yet been made known. But we know that when Christ appears, we shall be like him, for we shall see him as he is.

All who have this hope in him purify themselves, just as he is pure.

Everyone who sins breaks the law; in fact, sin is lawlessness.

But you know that he appeared so that he might take away our sins. And in him is no sin.

No one who lives in him keeps on sinning. No one who continues to sin has either seen him or known him.

Dear children, do not let anyone lead you astray. The one who does what is right is righteous, just as he is righteous.

The one who does what is sinful is of the devil, because the devil has been sinning from the beginning. The reason the Son of God appeared was to destroy the devil's work.

Chapter 1

A Safe Place

In the beautiful mid-west where you can see the sun rise from hundreds of miles due to the magnificent mass of flat lands that traverse acres and acres of farmland. This is where many farmers raise livestock to sale to their local community. For some reason, livestock and other animals grew healthy and strong on these farms. On a very large farm carved out in the middle of all the flatland was a farmer who had one focus and desire and that is to raise prize winning chickens.

The farmer built this huge honeycomb wire fence with 12 feet posts from end of his farm to the other end so that his chickens couldn't squeeze out through the wire fence and to prevent other large or small animals from getting in. However, some animals would dig under the fence so the farmer would periodically walk around to check the perimeter.

This particular farmer has won more 1st place awards for his chickens than any other farmer in the mid-west. His secret was providing them with fresh clean water and the best "chicken feed" money could buy. All his chicken were free ranged chickens. They had acres of land to walk, run, flutter, play, and just enjoy the day before they retire for the night in their carefully built one of kind chicken coops. The farmer spare no cost in raising and caring for his chickens. And for icing on the cake he dug out a beautiful crystal-clear pond for his chickens to play in and to cool off during the heat of the summer months.

His chickens produced some of the most healthy and colorful chicks grown in that part of the country. The farmer enjoyed walking round looking at his new baby chicks and while they just went about their day having fun with one another. It was an absolutely beautiful site to see. The farmer treated them like family, in fact, they were his family. So much that he would give all his chickens and chicks names based on their bright beautiful colors. He would also talk with them after the sun set late in the evening. The farmer spent hours talking to his chicks. Many of the other farmers would say his chicks understand him; and it was if the farmer understood them as well. You could only imagine what they were saying to each other.

Imagine the farmer walking around talking to his chickens and chicks. Telling them how beautiful they are and how the community depends on them for producing the best eggs they could produce. And the chickens would reply saying thanks Mr. Farmer for taking such good care of us. We have plenty of food, clean water, and a warm place to sleep at night. The other chickens would all join in the conversation offering thanks to the farmer. The little baby chicks would play and have fun with each other kicking up dirt, laughing and joking with each other.

During certain times of the year when the weather is really bad the farmer would get very concerned about some of other large birds flying over the fence and building bird nest in the chicken coops. He was really fearful of other wild animals breaking in the fence and killing his chickens for food. So, the farmer had to be very watchful and check every so often to make sure there were no other nests from other birds and animals in his coops. He had so many that he couldn't always find them. Every once in a while, he would fine another nest.

CHAPTER 1

2 Corinthians 5:17

Therefore, if anyone is in Christ, the new creature has come: The old has gone, the new is here!

Chapter 2

Family Woes

On one particular day the farmer noticed several new baby chicks. They were struggling to walk down the coop stairs on to the ground where the food bin was located. It was almost if they were yarning and rubbing their tiny eyes from the bright morning sun. The farmer just smiled and said, come down little baby chicks and take your time. We have plenty of food for you.

He noticed one of the chicks was a bit larger than the other chicks. It had larger claws, a funny looking yellow beak with large nostrils and unusually large wings. It's body appeared to be much larger and its feathers perfectly and evenly colored dark brown and had a beautiful white tail. His head was covered with bright white feathers. It looked like a white marshmellow. The farmer thought to himself as he had in time past…..just another unfortunate baby chick developing too fast and will not live to be a full-grown chicken. He thought to himself that one of his hens laid a bad egg. But he always treated them with the same care and respect as the rest but each morning he would anticipate not seeing that one playing with the rest of the chicks. He figured that particular one would die in a few days or so. He would wake up each morning prepared to clean the coop and remove the unfortunate chick from the coop. The farmer really hated losing his chicks. He really loved them all.

CHAPTER 2

The other chicks would make fun of those that were very different from them. This particular one was very different from the chicks. Most of the chicks start off looking and acting the same way. But this particular chick was different in every way from the beginning. This made the farmer sad so he decided he would give him a name also even though he didn't expect him to live very long and because it seems to make them all perk up.

The farmer was a Christian and enjoyed listening to gospel music. One of his favorite songs was "Amazing Grace". So, he decided to name this particular chick Amazing Grace. He was everything but graceful.

As time pass by the little baby chicks begin to grow, look, and act like full grown chickens. Quickly running from one side of the yard to the other side with their neck plunging back and forth. Flapping their wings conjuring up dust and dirt as if they were going to take flight.

After a few more weeks, to the pleasant surprise of the farmer his very special chicken Amazing Grace continued to grow and got healthier and stronger than the other chickens. However, the other chickens continue to tease him because of the way he looked.

Oh, how they tease him about his wings, yellow beak, and marshmellow head. They would laugh and tell jokes about him. They all called him the clumsy clown because of his huge yellow beak, white marshmellow head, and large claws. They also teased him about his appetite.

They would say....we better rush to eat before Amazing Grace eat up everything. His stomach is a bottomless pit. They constantly teased him and begin to totally reject him.

Amazing Grace did everything he could to fit in. He even laugh at all of their very bad jokes about him. The farmer could see the sadness on Amazing Grace face. He felt so sorry for him and didn't know what to do.

It had gotten so bad that the other chickens didn't want Amazing Grace around and wouldn't play with him anymore because he would mistakenly knock them down with his huge body. And so, they just laugh at him every day.

Amazing Grace became an outcast to everyone.

The farmer didn't know what to do. Amazing Grace was not laying any eggs but was eating most of the food. He was at a lost for a solution.

Then one day the farmer observed Amazing Grace sitting on a fence all alone looking up at the sky. The Farmer noticed this very large bird circling around in the sky above Amazing Grace. The farmer had noticed this large bird many times before but didn't give it much thought. But today he noticed the large bird coming down lower and lower as if he was looking at Amazing Grace. Then suddenly the large bird would then climb higher and higher until it couldn't be seen. The farmer said…wow…what a beautiful site? This happened day after day.

CHAPTER 2

Hebrews 9:12. *"He did not enter by means of the blood of goats and calves; but he entered the Most Holy Place once for all by his own blood, thus obtaining eternal redemption."*

Chapter 3

Keep your head up

Since Amazing Grace was too big to play with the chickens, Amazing Grace would come out every day to watch that large bird soar and glide across the sky with little, or no effort, barely flapping its wings. The other chicken would tease him and say…. you think you can do that? Well you can't! You are a chicken just like us so stop dreaming. In fact, you are handicapped…they joked. Amazing Grace would bow his head down to the dirt and eat a little food and then walk back to the chicken coop. And the other chickens would laugh, kicking dirt on him, calling him clumsy.

Again, the very next day the large bird would appear at the exact time Amazing Grace would come outside. This went on for weeks at a time. Amazing Grace begin to ignore the other chickens and just held his head high to the sky and watched the large bird.

One day Amazing Grace was being chased by the other chickens but they couldn't catch him because he was bigger and much, much faster. And as he was running Amazing Grace flapped his wings just a little and the air lifted him up a little higher than usual and he landed at the very top of the 12-foot fence post. The other chickens couldn't believe what he did. They begin to say, "how did you do that"? That's impossible! Several of the chickens took a

CHAPTER 3

running start and tried to get up enough flight to land on the other post but could only get a few feet off the ground. The other chickens begin to say to Amazing Grace…that was just luck. You caught the wind at the right time. I dare you to do it again. Come on down we dare you. But Amazing Grace just ignored them until they all walked away.

Looking down at what had just happened the large bird came down slowly in complete control, full of grace and balance made a landing on top of the other 12-foot post right next to Amazing Grace. They were only a few feet away from each other. But out of fear Amazing Grace panicked and leaped down off the post ran across the dirty yard, flapping it's wings flinging dirt everywhere. He finally reached the chicken coop where he went inside and hid in his nest. The large bird quickly took flight and after a while disappeared in the beautiful, heavenly blue sky.

With the orange sun going down you could view the majestic mountains that set high above the clouds appearing to dominate the skylight with array of snow cap peaks. They were miles away but on any given day you could easily see for miles and miles across the plains to the mountain tops. It was a breath-taking view.

The next day the large bird appeared again and Amazing Grace saw the large bird gliding in the sky with his large wings. Amazing Grace remembered what he was able to do the day before and took off running again to see if he could catch another wind to lift him on top of the post. Little did he know that the wind he was hoping to catch to lift him up was created by himself. So, suddenly he was off the ground and gracefully landed on the exact same post.

Day after day both Amazing Grace and the large bird repeated their routine. Amazing Grace would land on the 12-foot post and the large bird would circle around as if he was applauding for his success and Amazing Grace would stand on its' back claws and spread and flap his extremely large wings as to be taking a bow.

Each day the large bird would come down closer and closer but not to cause alarm to Amazing Grace. And finally, he decided to again land on the post next to him. This time Amazing Grace wasn't alarmed. He stayed and admired the large bird. The other chickens took note of the two of them sitting quietly on the post gazing in the sky. Moments later the large bird took flight and soon disappeared into the sunset.

Amazing Grace leaped off the post to the ground while all the chickens starred in ah. They asked him……what was that all about? Do you not know that large bird could kill you" …yeah, that's right, some of the other chickens echoed…? Watch yourself and stay off the post before you get injured. Stay down here on the ground with us where it is safe. You are a chicken and not a bird. You are one of us and will always be one of us. Don't fool yourself. We are going to tell Mr. Farmer about this. He will lock you up inside the chicken coop if you don't stop.

Chapter 4

Change is coming

That night when all the chickens were in their nest and ready for a good night rest, Amazing Grace laid restless in his nest. He kept thinking about the large bird and why it landed next to him on the post. He soon fell peacefully to sleep with his last thought "what is it like up there in the sky".

Early the next morning all the chickens marched out to the yard to start their daily routine of running around in the yard, eating and joking about Amazing Grace. They did not realize they were living in a "RUT". Whenever you do the same thing over and over again, you are in a RUT. He is normally the last one to exit the chicken coop because he is so large now and he could barely get out. In fact, he was beginning to get too large to stay inside the coop with the other chickens. They begin to complain to the farmer but the farmer didn't want to build a separate coop just for Amazing Grace. He thought that Amazing Grace is already costing him too much money and to build another coop would be very costly and Amazing Grace has never produced any eggs nor any baby chicks.

The farmer slowly walked over to Amazing Grace and told him he does not know what he is going to do with him. He just doesn't fit in and may he have to leave the farm soon. Amazing Grace held his head down and slowly walked over to the corner of the fence and sat on the ground and started to cry. He was really far away from the Farmer and all the other chickens. He just wanted to be alone.

Out for the daily routine the large bird noticed that Amazing Grace was not sitting on the post. He finally spotted him all alone sitting on the ground with his head down in the far corner of the fence. So, the large bird swooped down to the ground directly in front Amazing Grace only a few feet away. Amazing Grace was so sad that he wasn't alarmed by the large bird. So, the large bird walks slowly over to Amazing Grace and asked….is there something wrong? Amazing Grace told the large bird about his conversation with the farmer. The farmer stated that he doesn't know what he was going to do with me.

The large bird asked if he had a name….and he said…I am Amazing Grace. The large bird smiled and said…. that is an awesome name. Amazing Grace, said yes…. but what good is that going to do me now? The only reason why I have this name is because I am so different from the other chickens the farmer felt sorry for me and gave me that name to help me feel better. Can't you see how I look? I am so big and clumsy. And so, the large bird laugh….and said…. yes indeed. You are very different but you will be just fine. Don't worry about anything. You only need "Revelation Knowledge".

Amazing Grace asked…what is that? I have never heard of "Revelation Knowledge". The large bird said….it is really very simple…."if you deny someone of the knowledge of who they are you can make them to be whatever you want them to be; but if you teach them their heritage and culture, they will aspire to be greater than all those before them." Amazing Grace asked, what kind of talk is this? I have no idea what you are taking about. I am a chicken. I live with other chickens. I eat chicken food. I live in a chicken coop, and the chicken coop is inside of a fence. The large bird said….it is true that you live with other chickens, it is true that you live in a chicken coop, and it is true that you live in a fence. And it is definitely true that you look a

CHAPTER 4

lot different from the other chickens but it is not true that you are a chicken.

"if you deny someone of the knowledge of who they are you can make them to be whatever you want them to be; but if you teach them their heritage and culture, they will aspire to be greater than all those before them."

Romans 6:2
God forbid. How shall we, who died to sin live any longer in it?

Chapter 5

It's Ok to be different

A mazing Grace looked at the large bird as if he was crazy.…. He frankly got rather upset with the large bird and said.…. How dare you make fun of me. I get teased enough from my chicken friends if that is what you want to call them. I don't need you to make fun of me also. Leave me alone.…. Just leave me alone.

The large bird asked.…. Can we meet here tomorrow about the same time? I have something I want to show you. Amazing Grace said why… you want to make fun of me some more? Where am I going? Like you said, I live in a fence and I can't get out. I am not going anywhere so sure, come by tomorrow. The large bird quickly took flight and was soon in the clouds heading towards the mountains.

Later that night, Amazing Grace was thinking about how he just had an awful day. All his chickens friends made jokes and laugh at him. They told the farmer Amazing Grace doesn't belong here and he should kick him out of the chicken coop. The farmer felt sorry for Amazing Grace but he knew that the chickens were right. He had to tell Amazing Grace he may have to leave. Wow, what a big blow and sad news. And not to mentioned that his new friend just told him he wasn't a chicken. Amazing Grace was hurting so bad.

CHAPTER 5

Tears begin to flow down his face. He felt so all alone and thought, no one wanted to be his friend. No one cared about his feelings. He said to himself, it is not my fault I was born different. He was desperate and wanted to die. So, he decided that he would meet his friend tomorrow and tell him he was going to kill himself since he doesn't belong to anyone or anywhere.

Amazing Grace cried himself to sleep. Early the next morning all the chickens woke up and headed out to start their routine. Amazing Grace feared walking towards the door. He knew that he was very close to breaking one of the walls to the coop and definitely will not be able to get back in the coop after he exit. He manages to squeeze through once again but had no doubt that he couldn't ever return to the coop and will have to sleep outside.

His chicken friends laugh themselves to tears watching him squeezing and crawling out of the chicken coop. They joked and laughed so very hard. They all gathered around and continue laughing and joking, calling him all kinds of names. They begin to throw some of their food at him. They kicked dirt in his face. Amazing Grace ran over to his corner and they yielded at him don't ever come back you clumsy ox. You don't belong here.

Amazing Grace just wanted his life to be over. He was absolutely done. This would be the day he would end it all. Nothing was going to change his mind. No one loved him nor wanted him. He didn't fit in anywhere.

A few minutes later, Amazing Grace slowly raised his head and looked up into the sky and saw four large birds just like the one that made a visit to him yesterday. He thought, wow.... My new friend went and brought some of his friends back here to make fun of me also. He saw one of the large birds begin to come down from the sky towards the ground. It was his new friend. He landed right in front of Amazing Grace and said.... How are you? Amazing Grace feeling really bad said.... How do you think? What did you do, bring some of your friends here to make fun of me? The large bird said no...but I want you to meet them.

Ephesians 2:5-8

*Even when we were dead in trespasses, made us alive together with Christ (by grace you have been saved), **6** and raised us up together, and made us sit together in the heavenly places in Christ Jesus, **7** that in the ages to come He might show the exceeding riches of His grace in His kindness toward us in Christ Jesus. **8** For by grace you have been saved through faith, and that not of yourselves; it is the gift of God.*

Chapter 6

Joy cometh in the morning

Amazing Grace bowed his head down like a chicken and started to weep. He told the large bird what happened this morning and that he couldn't take it anymore. That he was going to end it all that night. The large bird said…look at me Amazing Grace…. Look at me. Lift your head up and look at me. Amazing Grace slowly raised his head while wiping the tears from his face. The large bird repeated himself…. What do you see? Amazing Grace said, what do you mean…what do I see? The large bird said, it is time for you to learn who you are. You remember I mentioned that to you….? Amazing Grace said yes, I remember. The large bird said what do you see? Amazing Grace said, I see you…. Tell me what you see…. The large bird repeated again. Amazing Grace said…. Well…I see a large bird with a big white head, with big black and white feathers, large wings and large claws on your feet.

The large bird said now walk over here with me and look into the pond and tell me what you see. Amazing Grace nervously leaned over into the pond and looked down to glean at his reflection. He said, I see a large bird with a big white head with black and white feathers, large wings and large claws on my feet. Amazing Grace said…. I look like you. The large bird said…that's right, you look like me. You are my son. The son of the most powerful bird

God ever created. Who is God…..he asked? God is our creator.

Amazing Grace said…what are you telling me? The large bird said…. Look up in the sky…those large birds up there are your family. Your mother, your brother and sister. I am your father. You are my son…. Born to soar in the deepest of the bluest sky. You are the most powerful bird in all creation. You are of me and I am of you. You can fly to the highest heights. You can soar where no other birds can even imagine. We live in the mountains above the horizon so we can see far across this beautiful land for miles and miles. I have been watching you for months waiting for this very special day. You are not a chicken you are an EAGLE. This land most admired bird that ever took flight. You are my child, my son, you are perfect.

With tears falling from his eyes his father wrapped his wings around him and he said I love you son and we missed you, it is time to come home.

Amazing Grace filled with tears and emotions asked, how did I get here? Why are you just now coming for me? Where have you all been all this time? Amazing Grace was filled mixed emotions. On one hand he was experiencing intense joy from the news but fearful and still filled with rejection, sadness and pain.

With his head bowed down to the ground he heard and felt a gust of wind forcing him to wrap his large wings over his face to cover his eyes from the dust. He raised his head to see what was happening, he saw 3 other eagles, his family, descending down from the sky. They drew closer and closer then gracefully landed alongside of their father. For the first time he met his mother, older brother and sister. Amazing Grace said excitingly, they look like me too. They all giggled and then lovely embraced him.

Amazing Grace asked his mother how he ended up on the farm. His mother told him that one night she and his family was traveling back home when a huge storm came from nowhere. The wind was very powerful and the

CHAPTER 6

rain came down like a blanket. His mother continued…..I was carrying you as a baby egg and I didn't want to risk trying to fly above the storm under those conditions. Normally, we fly way above the storms but we couldn't take that chance with you. You are very precious, special, and we love you dearly. So, we had to sacrifice some time from you in order to make sure you were safe and could spend the rest of your life with us. Your father spotted this wonderful chicken farm and decided this would be the best place for me to give birth to you. While your brother and sister flew above the storm, your father and I traverse the wind and rain landed safely near the chicken coop. Your father kept watch while I barely squeezed in the chicken coop without disturbing the other chickens. There, I found an empty nest with fresh hay. There you were laid and covered with hay. I stayed as long as I could but we had to leave before the sun came up.

Amazing Grace's father said, your mother didn't want to leave you behind but she knew it was the best for you so she covered you with hay and slipped out of the chicken coop. We flew up above the clouds and storm to join your brother and sister and headed home to the mountains where we live.

I came back here every day and watched you grow bigger and stronger. His father laugh…..yes, you had a very big appetite compared to the other chickens. You couldn't see me at first because I flew above the clouds. But as you grew bigger and older I came down to get a closer look at our awesome son. Your mother and siblings couldn't wait for me to return every day with the news of how you were doing. We all were so excited and knew it wouldn't be long before you would be joining us.

I am so sorry son we had to leave you here but you are too important to us for us to take a chance on losing you in that storm. Storms comes and go but we will always be with you.

Romans 4:1-7

*What then shall we say that Abraham our father has found according to the flesh? **2** For if Abraham was justified by works, he has something to boast about, but not before God. **3** For what does the Scripture say? "Abraham believed God, and it was accounted to him for righteousness." **4** Now to him who works, the wages are not counted as grace but as debt. **5** But to him who does not work but believes on Him who justifies the ungodly, his faith is accounted for righteousness, **6** just as David also describes the blessedness of the man to whom God imputes righteousness apart from works: **7** "Blessed are those whose lawless deeds are forgiven, And whose sins are covered;*

Chapter 7

We have another home

Are you ready to go home? Amazing Grace said yes…. I am so ready but how will I get there. His father said, you now have "Revelation Knowledge" that changes things. You know who you are, the son of the most powerful bird on the earth capable of flying higher than any creature ever made by our creator. You have all you need now. Just **BELIEVE**! I can't do this for you. You have to do it for yourself. I **LOVE** you; I am very **PROUD** of you; and I have **FAITH** in you son.

Amazing Grace wiped the tears from his eyes and lifted up his head. You could see him starting to believe every word of his father. He took a deep breathe as if the revelation of who he is began to register. It was if he filled himself with power, faith, courage, and pride. And then he exhaled as if he was blowing out all the doubt, negative thoughts, and low self esteem that kept him from becoming the creation that God intended him to be.

Now by this time all the chickens were watching and the farmer came out to see what was going on. His father took a few steps and quickly elevated to the sky with the rest of his family looking back at Amazing Grace as if he was saying…. you can do it son…you can do it.

I AM AMAZING GRACE

The farmer approached Amazing Grace asked if he was alright. Amazing Grace yes, I am awesome, I am amazing, I am delivered, I am redeemed, I am saved, I am blessed, I wonderful, I am loved, I am the child of the most powerful bird that the creator had ever made. The farmer's eyes were as bright as a light. The other chicken said you are clumsy, you are a chicken.

He pointed to the sky and said there is my family. I am an EAGLE. I know who I am. Watch me soar. His family came down from the clouds so he could see them clearly. They hovered around to watch Amazing Grace take flight. Amazing Grace said to the farmer….thanks for everything you did for me. I will never forget you. Then he said with a very nervous voice to the farmer and the other chickens, stand back. Amazing Grace begin to run and flap his wings as hard as he could and took flight for a few feet but quickly came crashing down. All the chickens begin to laugh but the farmer said…I have always known you were special. You can do it. I believe in you too. The chickens continue to laugh…. saying you are a chicken, just a chicken. Amazing Grace took off again running, with head down, flapping his huge wings, and only took flight for a few feet and crashed again, and again.

Finally, Amazing Grace looked up at his family and they could see him looking up at them and suddenly he could see them clearly and closer. His telescopic vision came into focus like a laser. His nostril opened like windpipes and his lungs filled with air. His chest protruded out and his wing span were fully extended. He took off running again but this time his head was looking up with his eyes focused on his father. He could see his father smiling, he could see the tears in his mother's eyes and he could hear his brother and sister saying you can do it brother….you can do it. And without hesitation he lifted his feet off the ground flapping his wings creating a wind tunnel that lifted him higher and higher. He kept his head up to the sky where he saw his father. He continued to climb until he reached his family and they all circle around him and then they dove down towards the farm as to say thank you to the farmer for taking care of my son Amazing Grace. The family climbed higher and higher until the chickens and the farmer couldn't see them anymore.

CHAPTER 7

As the farmer gazed at the Eagles flying into the sunset, he started singing his favorite song........

Amazing Grace, how sweet the sound, that saved a wretch like me; I was lost, but now am found. T'was blind but now I see, T'was Grace that taught my heart to fear and Grace, my fears relieved, how precious did that grace appear. The hour I first believed, through many dangers, toils, and snares, We have already come. T'was grace that brought us safe thus far and grace will lead us home, And.....

Romans 4:13-16

For the promise that he would be the heir of the world was not to Abraham or to his seed through the law, but through the righteousness of faith. **14** *For if those who are of the law are heirs, faith is made void and the promise made of no effect,* **15** *because the law brings about wrath; for where there is no law there is no transgression.* **16** *Therefore it is of faith that it might be according to grace, so that the promise might* *be sure to all the seed, not only to those who are of the law, but also to those who are of the faith of Abraham, who is the father of us all...*

Epilogue

Revelation Knowledge Changes Things! So, Change

Like the eagle "Amazing Grace" many Christians today do not know who they are and the FREE gifts that comes with the salvation and promise of God.

Don't believe the lies of the enemy (satin/devil). He wants you to think that you are saved but you have to earn you way to be Sanctified, Redeemed, Holy, and Righteous.

The enemy knows that if we as the body of Christ is constantly working to earn these gifts then we are not growing the Kingdom of God by sharing the Gospel. Also, the enemy want us to be disabled to share the Gospel due to the self-condemnation that we place on ourselves.

When we "feel" not worthy to share the Gospel because of our past, present, and/or future sins the enemy is winning. Yes, we sin but we are no longer Sinners. The enemy knows he can't do anything about your eternal life and Salvation with God/Jesus Christ but he can make us ineffective Christians by disabling us from sharing the Gospel with others.

You are worthy. You are no longer a "sinner" – yes… you may still be sinning but you are no longer a "Sinner" in God's eye. You are a Spirit Being that is living in a broken/sin body. You are living in an imperfect and sinful world. You are being tempted and tested by the enemy; but you are a new creature. The old creature/sinner is dead.

You are a citizen of Heaven where the streets are made of gold. You are here on earth as God's Ambassador to share the Gospel of Jesus Christ.

No matter what, you are still the child of the Most High God and the devil is a liar and the father of lies.

Now you have "Revelation Knowledge". Allow it to sink in your Spirit. Like Amazing Grace, now that you know who you are, take flight and be all you can be. Don't be afraid or ashamed to share this good news. Exercise your faith. God loves you…..I said God loves you….just the way you are and there is nothing you can do to change that. Hallelujah!

"For God so loved the world that he gave his one and only begotten Son, that whoever believes in him shall not perish but have eternal life". John 3:16. Think about that for a minute. This is the kind of love that only God can give.

God Bless and keep you forever…. "It is impossible to know what you do not know, but now you know".

Other books by Dr. Honney Lavern Barner

We invite you to continue your journey with the "Behind the Door Series." Once you start reading you will not want to put it down. This series is movie bound.

I AM AMAZING GRACE

#1 New Release amazon **Best Seller amazon** **Most Gifted Book amazon**

Best Selling Author Dr. Honney Lavern Barner is one of the most dynamic, exciting, and refreshing author in the literary industry today. He is an amazing talent that captivates his audiences with his energy, warmth, humor, and genuine compassion for the Gospel of Jesus.

What people are saying about Behind the Door and Behind the Door I & II.

"Honney Lavern Barner is a man who has walked a path of continual growth and self discovery, and as a result he continues to grow his impact on the world. From a career in the United States Armed Forces, to a successful entrepreneurial career to a successful speaking and training career and now to writing a powerful novel…he never stops going or growing! Read this book and get ready to be uplifted and inspired!"

-**Dr. Willie Jolley, Hall of Fame Speaker, Host of the Willie Jolley Show on Sirius XM and Best Selling Author of "A Setback Is A Setup For A Comeback."**

"Honney Lavern Barner's book chronicles an amazing spiritual journey not unlike his own. It is a powerful story told by a masterful storyteller, and has a number of applications to modern day life. In this age of spiritual uncertainty, "Behind the Door" provides guidance for the believer and skeptic alike, and hope that there is indeed a higher power at work."

-**William Faucette, Entrepreneur, Former CEO and Success Coach.**

If you ever wondered if you could start you very own business in the Network Marketing Industry then you need to read "Let's Be Honest" about MLM/Network Marketing". Some say Dr. Honney Lavern Barner with his 40+ years of experience and success in this industry is the leading expert in world today. And he is right here in the DMV. Wow!

He is also passionate about sharing the Gospel of Jesus Christ especially to our youth. He desire for them to know "now" what take most people a life to realize. We are children of the Most High God – Saved, Holy, Redeemed, Righteous, and filled with the Holy Spirit. Every youth need to read this powerful life changing message and you should too. And if you ever thought about earning additional income through a home business he is one of the leading experts.

Get your copies by visiting: www.drhlbarner.com. Share with your family and friends. Post on FB, Twitter, Instagram, and other sides. Let's celebrate our local author!

www.drhlbarner.com

How you can help spread the word?

- Receive an update on the Behind the Door Series adventure to reach the New York Times Best seller and movie offers. Register your email address with us today.
- Purchases additional copies of Behind the Door and share with your family and friends. Provide your thoughts about "What if there is No God and What if there is a God? Help me expand this global conversation. Share with Churches, Book Clubs, Homes, Families, Universities, Seminaries, and other organizations.
- Tune in to Dr. Honney Lavern Barner's Hour of Power (HoP) weekly Podcast. Discussions about Behind the Door Series – What if there was no God and What if there is a God?
- Visit our Facebook page, Twitter, Instagram, and LinkedIn.
- Visit drhlbarner.com to read my recent blog, My Faith, Radio Show, Books, Author Information and much more. Don't forget to leave your email address.
- Sign up for my monthly newsletter.
- Message the Author and get updates on Behind the Door Series
- Post your thoughts, insights, and testimonies about Behind the Door Series on all your Social Media resources.
- Read what others around the world are saying about the Behind the Door Series.
- All the profits from the sale of my novels will be used to fund the movie "Behind the Door". Please order the entire Behind the Door Series. Help me raise funds to produce a movie by hosting fundraising events anywhere and everywhere.

Word of Mouth Matters - Your Help Matters

Our goal for Behind the Door Series is to become #1 on the New York Times Bestseller's list simply by inspired, passionate, and motivated readers and supporters spreading the word about this life changing novel.

Our goal for I AM AMAZING GRACE is get this book into the hands of our youth so that they learn early in their life they are children of the most high God and because of what Jesus Christ did on the cross they are Saved, Redeemed, Holy, and Righteous. Not to waste time trying to earn those gifts but simply share the Gospel of Jesus Christ.

We need your help in spreading the word to everyone you know and everyone you don't know. Here are some ideas on how you can help get the word out to your circle of friends.

Talk about "Behind the Door" on **Email, Twitter, Instagram, Facebook, You Tube, Messenger,** and **Blogs**. Host discussion forums you visit, and other places you engage other people on the Internet. I am not asking you to post advertisements, simply share your thoughts on how after reading it, made you feel and share the link to" Behind the Door" website.

Purchase a few books as gifts and donate them to churches, shelters, prisons, rehabilitation homes, and other places where people may need to be encouraged about their faith.

WORD OF MOUTH MATTERS - YOUR HELP MATTERS

If you own a small business please consider putting a display of this novel on your counter to resell to customers. We offer discounts for resale for orders of 10 or more novels.

If you have a **Website, Blog, You Tube Channel**, etc. please consider sharing "Behind the Door" and tell them how it impacted you and your faith. Don't tell them how the story ends but do give them the link to the website - **www.drhlbarner.com.**

Write a **book review and publish it in your local newspaper, magazine, or website.** Contact your local radio, podcast or TV station to have the author on their show.

Give "Behind the Door" as a gift for **Birthdays, Christmas, Anniversaries, Fundraisers, Give-a-ways** and other events where gifts and prizes are expected.

Make recommendations to community groups, church groups, book clubs, and others to have the author as their guest speaker at your **Conventions, Seminars, Expos, Festivals, and other gatherings.**

Use "Behind the Door" for **Small groups discussions at your local Church and Book clubs.** The author would be honored to make a surprise appearance.

Insights to Upcoming
  Behind the Door III: "Welcome to Heaven" Release in 2021

At this point, *Behind the Door III* – Welcome to Heaven will provide insights to what happens to you when you go to sleep and journey to Heaven.

Behind the Door IV -Revelation Unleashed will follow the actual book of Revelation through the eyes of "John" as written.

What would you like to know about falling asleep and transitioning to Heaven?

Who and what will you see?

Behind the Door IV: "Revelation Unleashed" Release in 2022

The *Behind the Door IV* begins with God telling Jonathan that it is time for his Son, Jesus Christ return to Earth to gather the Church and prepare the Earth for His eternal dwelling place.

Will Jonathan be the modern "John" from the book of Revelation?

What will God allow Jonathan to see? Is this the actual end of the Earth as we know it?

What will be unleashed upon the Earth? What is happening upon the Earth that has angered God to this end?

Follow Dr. Honney Lavern Barner on Social Media

I AM AMAZING GRACE

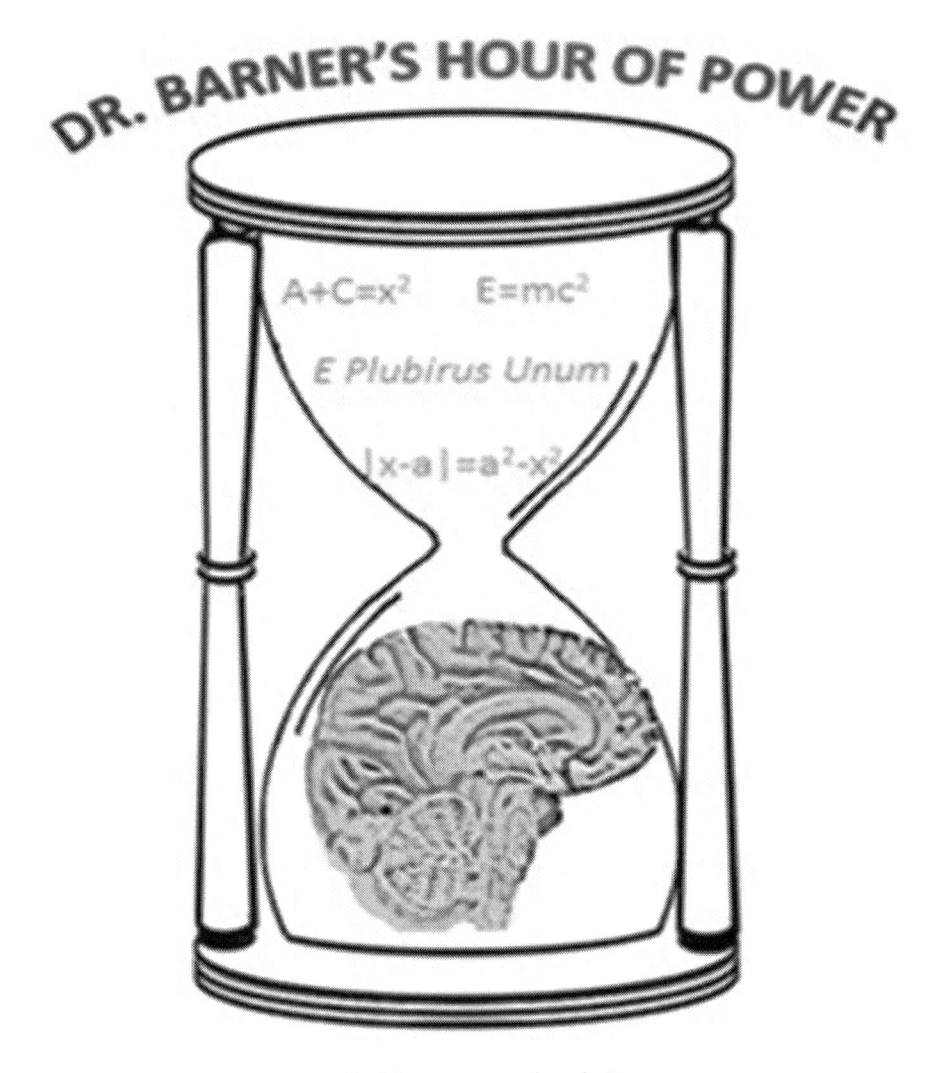

DR. BARNER'S HOUR OF POWER

$A+C=x^2$ $E=mc^2$

E Plubirus Unum

$|x-a|=a^2-x^2$

God loves you and so do I.

Facebook, Instagram, Twitter, and YouTube
  Website: www.drhlbarner.com

Made in the USA
Columbia, SC
23 September 2020